# Silver Witch Rose
## Ellie Ann Deighton

Copyright © 2025 by Ellie Ann Deighton

All rights reserved.

No part of this publication may be reproduced, distributed, or transmitted in any form or by any means, including photocopying, recording, or other electronic or mechanical methods, without the prior written permission of the publisher, except as permitted by Australian copyright law. For permission requests or bulk orders, contact the author.

The story, all names, characters, and incidents portrayed in this production are fictitious. No identification with actual persons (living or deceased), places, buildings, and products is intended or should be inferred.

Book Cover by Ellie Ann Deighton

1st Edition 2025

# Contents

| | |
|---|---|
| Epigraph | 1 |
| Ellie's Silver | 2 |
| Dedication | 4 |
| Foreword | 7 |
| You Caught Her | 11 |
| 1. The competing witch. | 29 |
| 2. The defeat of the witch. | 73 |
| 3. The discreet witch. | 87 |
| 4. The teacher witch. | 105 |
| 5. The evil witch. | 125 |
| 6. The wise witch. | 133 |
| 7. The silver witch rose. | 141 |
| Queen Of The Stones | 145 |
| salt sugar spirit | 149 |
| About the author | 151 |
| Author's note | 153 |

| | |
|---|---|
| The Remembering | 155 |
| Acknowledgements | 157 |

*Silver Witch Rose* is a journey to accepting your magic
And its place in the village
And rising into the calling
To share your natural talent
Whilst receiving the talents of others
Because we are remembering
We weren't born to live alone

When the spirit of the high priestess, the coven leader has swept through us and all we see are fellow humans with a soul doing their best, yearning for connection, flailing and unsure how, and we can see that the 'how' doesn't matter, their nature does and we love that. That love. That higher love is when we have found the silver.
~ evidence suggests

ALSO OF ELLIE'S SILVER

FICTION
Ankhara Codes I: An Adventure to Essence
Ankhara Codes II: Allies of the Soul
Ankhara Codes III: A Devotion To Peace

ORACLE CARDS
Fruits of the Feminine

POETRY
'It' is GOLD
Fire Body Warm
Water River Run

NON-FICTION
Myths of a Mystic Woman

JOURNAL
Creatively Loving

MUSIC ALBUMS
Temple Calling: An Album For Your Altar

ONLINE TRAININGS & COURSES:
Intuitively Me: The Wheel of Life

more at elliedeighton.com

This is the third book of seven in The Elemental Collection; a poetry series focused on the seven essential elements of fulfilment.

You can read The Elemental Collection in any order you choose.

*To all who ever sat in my circles,*
*And to the empty cushion for all who haven't found us yet,*
*And to Elissa for placing the empty cushion,*
*Thank you for choosing your silver,*
*May you rest and rise,*
*Bloom and shed,*
*Just as nature intended.*
*All my heart,*
*Ellie*

ELLIE ANN DEIGHTON

# Foreword

## In my journal I wrote...

April 9 2025

End result: To meet my muse and be informed of the calling of my heart.

I am the magic
And the muse
And I am here
To say to you:

When my spirit
Washes over
There will be
No ifs or buts
Simply oneness
Shedding
Remembering
A falling of the crust

You'll look into my eyes
In a sister, a lover, friend
And you'll right there remember
This is not the end.
It's not the first time either
Sure as it won't be the last
As we sit here together
We'll see shadows of times past
Some of them will glimmer
Like remembering old love
Others will make you shiver
As did the torturer's glove
But here we are together
We made it here to now
And all that really matters
Is we finally figured out
That circles are how we gather
With no end or tip or start
That circles are how we remember
The raven's wings will spread apart
And suddenly we're flying
High up in the sky
There's nothing we're surviving
Our head's are held up high
But right up there above them
Is a pulsing bright pink heart
The symbol of our oneness and love
The sun where it all starts

And here beside each other
We'll find brothers, lovers, friends
And finally, breathe a sigh of relief
The village didn't really end
We never really left
Our soul's were not forsaken
The village is right here
Our soul circle is here for the taking.

**Welcome to Silver.**

ELLIE ANN DEIGHTON

# You Caught Her
## The Prologue

The remembering
Came from underneath the earth
She was in the fields
And felt a sense of blossoming
So she reached down
Lost her fingers in the soil
Closed her eyes
Took a deep breath
If you were watching,
You would have caught your breath
In awe of her beauty
The breeze dancing through her hair
And the spirit of the Earth dancing towards
Her hands
And the seeds
In the field
Responding
Growing
Fed with a divine nourishment
Sprouting with a knowing
They were loved
Cherished
Depended upon
And the neighbours watched
But they didn't see beauty
They saw sorcery
And that wasn't a compliment,
Nor a recognition of her power

It was an accusation

An insult

*How could her lavender be more potent?*

*How could her seed grow more prolific?*

– She must be a witch

Defied by her connection to nature
Because they felt subject to it
They stormed in
Crossing the threshold
To her sanctuary
Her house
*Damn you, Witch!*
They yelled
Convinced further by the harvested flowers
Upside down to dry
In abundance because of her connection to the Earth
Colours so vibrant
Smells so strong
*Devil worshipper!*
Because the craft can only move through a man
And only in the name of the church
Or some other excuse
For it to be anything bar the simple powers of a woman
For this connection to be made wrong
For she had no husband
And no children
She was alone
No one to fight for her
No one to tell them they were wrong
*She isn't evil*
*She is love*
*She isn't competing with you*
*She would heal you as though her life depended upon it*

In a way it does
And she knows it
She knows we don't exist alone
She knows her crops could heal and feed and love
The whole village
And had she been given the chance
Had enough time passed
Had her generous spirit been given the opportunity
She would have shared
And of course
That too would have been a sin
An insult
How dare she be so abundant
And shake that abundance in the face of others
Mocking their failures
Poking holes in their pain
*She couldn't possibly be feeding the children from her goodness*
*She couldn't possibly be sharing for the sake of it*
*It's a manipulation*
*She is trying to trick us*
*It's a spell!*
*It's a curse!*
*If you consume her herbs she will syphon you and your crops will die as hers flourish!*
– And so the whole village was starved

It wasn't long
Before holding her hostage wasn't enough
Keeping her
In a hole in the ground
Wouldn't suffice
Torturing her
In her own filth
Which truly
She didn't so much mind
Being down in the earth
If it weren't for the cold
For she could befriend the worms
And she could embrace the soft arms of the soil
The thick strength in the roots
And the depth of story in the stones
The dirt underneath her fingernails
It was none of these things that bothered her
It was the throwing of fruit as her insult
The waste of food
The pure meanness for the sake of it
The accusation and assumed humiliation of her nature
The corruption of such beauty
The turning against her from her own village
She was a child here once
And suddenly they all forgot
Suddenly all they can see is that she is evil!
Suddenly, even with all the ones who have known her
From birth

Surrounding her
She is alone
Cast aside
Not because she is truly mad
Nor because she meant any harm
But because she was a woman
Alone
Doing well
Connected to the earth
Freely exhibiting her power
Willing to open her arms and share
And that is a dangerous thing
– The village feared her inner beauty

There was nothing she could do
Nothing she could say
To sway them
From their fear
Even if she had succeeded
With a small few
They would have told the others
*She bewitched them!*
And those who had wobbled in her conviction
Would have screamed
*She bewitched me!*
*Cleanse me, Priest!*
And they too would have been punished or protected
Depending on the mood
Because witchcraft didn't have to mean much
It just meant there was someone to silence
Threaten
Shrink
Shutdown
End
Disempower
So it wouldn't have mattered
What she did
– She still would have burned

## SILVER WITCH ROSE

Alas!
It did matter
To her spirit
For she was awake in her death
And so as her flesh burned
She did not
As her heart stopped
Her soul unleashed
The women cried
The men cheered
None of them knew why
None of their crops were better off
Her body was wasted
Her love neglected
The soil mourned not for her,
But for the village
– They freed her spirit and trapped their own

After the smell and smoke fade away
There stand the remains
The reminder
*It is not okay to be magic*
*Fuck magic*
*It is not okay to do well*
*You must not shine*
*Do not stand out*
*You must not enjoy the soil between your fingers*
*Hard work only will be rewarded here,*
*Appropriately,*
*Women will not succeed alone,*
*It is important for women to marry and mate,*
*Keep a good home,*
*But not too good,*
*And keep pretty,*
*But not beautiful,*
*Do not embrace your power,*
*This could be your future,*
*See the way the women turned upon her?*
*That could be your future,*
*See the way the men cheered?*
*This could be your future*
*Behave*
*Behave*
*Behave*
And so we learned, behave or burn
And the witch became an archetype

## SILVER WITCH ROSE

For everything that was ever hated
And everything that was ever feared
Trapped in a woman's body
– Still, the silver witch rose

On the ground
In the years that followed
A tree grew
More like a brush
And every year
On the first day of that fear-filled month,
A silver rose would bloom
And a child would love it
A mother would hush her
And so the cycle would continue
Until eventually
Many, many years later
One would look upon the rose and know love
– The witch's ever after

## SILVER WITCH ROSE

The witches come here
One by one
And pick the flower
One by one
And cast a spell
One by one
And open hearts
One by one
And maybe you caught her
Maybe you made her wrong
Maybe you laughed at her
Called her silly
Blamed her
Hated her
Envied her
But deep down
A seed was planted
When you saw her smell the rose
And you wanted the freedom
Whether you knew it or not
– And so your pursuit of the silver began

Are you a witch?

Are you a human?

Are you an elf?

Are you a frog?

Are you a maiden?

Are you an elder?

– Is there magic in your heart? (Yes and it is silver)

My grandmother once told me
Her mother was a witch
And many years later
I realised
She was my spirit teacher
And sometimes we make things up for fun
Or in the name of magic being real
But this connection
I couldn't make this up
It scared me
Shocked me into my skin
And that's how I knew it was real
It shocked me into my skin
Not out of it
The more I spoke to her
The more me I felt
And then I noticed
Similar expressions
Similar chosen words
Between my grandmother
And my great grandmother in spirit
Only after my best friend asked me
*Who is your spirit guide?*
Only then
Did I notice
This family magic is real
And though it may have been denied
And hidden

And called something else
And made make believe
And twisted over the years
Skipped a generation or three
That silver thread was right here
In me
– The silver thread landed in my heart

## SILVER WITCH ROSE

My grandmother says she isn't a witch
But she loves astrology
Sees the past and the future in the stars
– We can all call the silver different things

Maybe you caught her
Maybe she burns
Maybe she had a resurrection
Maybe she returns
– The silver witch lives

# The competing witch.

The witch was feared

So deeply

That no sister was safe

When I think of the past

I can feel the pain

Of knowing that you were entirely alone

That at the end of the day

It was

Every witch for themselves

Every woman for herself

Every man for himself

Everyone for themselves

And society doesn't work like that

That's why the village was broken

Because it broke the fragile hearts

Of everybody

To betray one another

To feel the certainty of betrayal

And I know there were incredible women

Incredible allies

Incredible feats of courage and love

Of course

But the overwhelming sense of the past

Is loss

And I can't help but notice

We wouldn't require a revolution of the village

Of women gathering

Of men gathering

Of people gathering
Of reminding each other that we're there for one another
Of asking for help
Of leaning on our loved ones
Of loving the mother postpartum
Of loving the entire family unit
If we didn't lose the silver thread
Or at least lose our grip on it
Because it didn't go anywhere
Our magic didn't leave
But our safety to express it sure did
And our ability to be celebrated certainly went away
And I can't help but wonder
What might be different?
What might our village look like today
If the witches weren't competing
If the women weren't competing
If the people weren't competing
For what they thought they knew as love
– If you have to beg for it, it isn't love and it sure ain't silver

I compete

Silently

With the person on the treadmill next to me

I wonder if they know

If we're both in on it

They're tracking my scores too

Or is this just my wound

My pain

Screaming

*You must win!*

*Don't be beaten!*

*It's first or last!*

And I'm still not sure

But I'm fitter for it

– Doing my best at being human doesn't mean I don't have silver

Sometimes all I have to offer
Is to remind myself I'm a human
And I'm hurting
And I'm still here
– I'm still filled with silver

Even when the hurt overcomes me
Even when my vision is blurred with tears
Even when my body aches to be still
Even when my sisters pommel me with junk
I am doing my best
I am filled with silver
I am remembering
I am filled with silver
– The ancestors stand in silver before me

The ancestors stand before me
Silver in their hands
Mostly
Some of them I see a silver thread
And it's different
It's going through them
More translucent
And I can tell
Ah,
They didn't express their silver
And they've passed now
And it's okay,
They become a lesson,
A soul teacher
To show me I can choose differently
I live in a time
Filled with expression
Encouraged expression
And also in a country
So obsessed with tearing others down
And in a world
So obsessed with making the unknown bad
And magic
Real magic
The silver thread
To most
Even though it is familiar
There is a reason the witch is on trend!

It is also terrifying
It is also a wound
It is also a responsibility
It is also a superpower
And you know in the movies all those with the superpowers have lost something
Well, I've lost you
– Searching for the silver thread in you all

SILVER WITCH ROSE

I hope you choose it

But it's none of my business

– It's up to you whether you live in your magic

I have a theory
A hypothesis of sorts
That all our hearts are filled with magic
And all of us learn to tape on the lid
And many of us are holding that lid down
Pressing down
As though our hearts are a cauldron
And if you keep the lid on tight
The smells won't trigger any alarms
The smoke won't rise
Your power won't make you a target
And we've all become so good
*Hide your magic*
*Laugh at your games*
*Wear the mask*
*Don't be silly*
*You're just being silly*
*Empower women, but hate them*
*Empower yourself, but hate you*
*Squash the magic in*
And the funny thing is
It matters not the cages we place our silver in
We will still long for the village
We will still carry the same gifts
We will still long for deep connection
We will still feel the call
– Silver speaks through iron cages

It won't matter

You can be the most disconnected

The most in denial

The most fearful

The most happy looking

It won't matter

When it comes to hearing the call

– Nothing can compete with the silver inside your heart (except you)

I suppose you can
Compete with the silver in your heart
You can ignore it
Turn it down
Pretend it isn't there
But one day
You'll grieve your silver
And maybe the pain will make you move
The silver will crack through
Your heart will break
You will remember yourself
You will see the silver light in others
You will no longer be obsessed with being separate
You will seek the circle
You will be looking for the witches
The weird
The wacky ones
The ones where you can entirely be yourself
And you may not call them witches
But remember
Witches are simply ones who connect with nature
And if you're letting yourself be weird,
If you're open to all your wackiness,
If you're loving the great outdoors
Or tending to flowers and houseplants
If you have deeply loving relationships
If you find yourself nourished to the bone with other people
It's highly likely

And you might not know it

But you're a witch

– Silver is in everybody

It looks different in everybody
The silver thread
Once you're trained to see it
The thread itself isn't changing
But the way she holds it
The way it opens him
The way they dance when they are one with it
Oh it's different
– The way you are silver is magic

And we can see each other's 'different'
And make it a tone we must compete
With
For
Against
But it should be an inspiration
Invitation
Instigation
Of us being our own 'different'
It's not a real competition
It can't be
You can never really compete at being me
I'll always win
I can never really compete at being you
You'll always win
Therefore the competition will always create losers
And it isn't necessary
Because we all carry the silver thread
We can all pull from it
Draw from it
Listen to it
Become one with it
And when we do we all win
– Silver living is life giving

When I set the altar
For a ritual
I feel the silver thread
As an ancestor piercing the veil
She pours through my arms
Reaching from my heart
Placing items in their place
Calling forth the ritual magick
There is no wrong position
You can't make a mistake
In this, your ritual
But oh
You can align it
You can learn from it
You can love it
And that's what happens
As though my hands know what my heart does
And I let it happen
I let them move
And a moment comes
My breath deepens
*There we are*
– Silver pulls everything into place

If I am threatened by your silver
I must be missing mine
I must have buried her again
Closed the lid of my heart cauldron
But I must remember
That even thinking of the silver
Even acknowledging it in her or him
Brings mine back to surface
Helps me feel like I might win
And you see the real competition isn't between me and you
It's between my ego and my heart
Between belief and presence
If I can notice I am threatened
I can also notice I have disappeared
No longer present
Grieving the past
Fearing the future
Against you
Not really here
And that can be enough to bring me back
– Noticing silver helps me notice the silver

I want to fight for you,
Not against you
– You have silver too

I want to be with you,
Not against you
– You are my village

I want to tell you,
Without fearing you
– I am scared of my village

## SILVER WITCH ROSE

I want to guide you,
Without everything being my fault
– Connect to your own silver, not just mine

It doesn't work

Doesn't help

Doesn't move you forward

If you connect to your teachers' silver

Your friends' silver

Your villages' silver

And abandon your own

– Silver isn't a one way thing

You compete with nature

When you don't listen to the winter

And choose not to rest

Do not lean into the nourishment of others

Do not ask for help

Try to do it all alone

Let yourself be depleted over and over

Empty yourself out in service to others

Tell yourself that you're being a good person,

Even though you're tired.

When you

Don't sleep

Don't eat well

Undernourish

Overcompensate with sugar

Call it hibernation when really you're just hiding

Hiding and hibernation are so different, dear witch.

You are meant to be with nature.

Your leaves are meant to fall off.

You are meant to sink deep into your bed,

Sleep for more hours when the days are shorter,

Rest more when the weather suggests it

And of course,

You can still have your physical excellence,

You can still train,

You can still do hard things,

You can still conquer challenges,

You can still be vulnerable,

And you aren't meant to always be doing this with an empty cup.

Winter is hard.

We know it.

Our mental health knows it.

Our DNA remembers it.

Surviving winter is a celebration,

But we can't celebrate if we don't even acknowledge that we are going through it.

If we just soldier on

There's no celebration

There's no making it

There's no other side

Because we carry the winter in our bones

The winter leaves us defeated

We are not one with the cycles in our skin

When we push, push, push all winter long

And then wonder why we aren't doing as well as we could be,

It is no wonder darling,

That if you do not rest,

You will not peak,

For it is only the trees that are harvested and pruned

That thrive in the following seasons

– Silver says we are not separate from the seasons, we are the seasons

When we hit spring
And we don't notice
We are competing with the innate wisdom
That tells us to be present
To pause
To notice
*'Hey, the flowers are arriving!'*
*'Wow, the snow is melting!'*
*'Persephone has risen!'*
Maybe you notice
But only to the level of your increased convenience
It's easier to drive now
Easier to get up in the mornings when there's a little sunshine
Warmer for your bones
Easier to see people when it is more enticing to go outside
But spring
Is the time to play
To stretch
To slowly rise from the deep nourishing rest
That winter brings out in us
To celebrate
The abundance returning
And the abundance we feel
For we have filled ourselves up from the middle
And we miss that
When we miss spring,
We miss the joy
Of the maiden

And the little boy who so innocently wishes to climb rocks
Now is the time
To do something for the sake of fun
Try something new
Share yourself a little more
Tend to your winter seeds
Maybe notice that in the darkest days of the year
You have received inspiration
Ideas came
You weren't maybe ready to act on them
But the life force energy is returning
Focus turns from soups to sudden bursts of energy
It's not summer yet
But the light is here
And so are you
And you are competing with nature
If you are still so, so tired from winter,
Still in spring pretending it's summer,
Because it cannot and will not be summer all year round,
The wheel it turns
And turns and turns
And you are ageing
You are maturing
You are developing
You are deepening your harvest
Only if you let nature have its way with you
Not as an excuse

But as a way to take care of all of you
– Silver says you are seasonal

Oh and then summer comes

Real summer

But you are so tired

Because there was no restful winter

And spring was not a slow incline

You have been go, go, go

Run, run, run

I don't know about you

(although I think I do)

But I cannot run all the time

At the moment I can run six kilometres

And then I need a rest

A drink of water

A little walk

Before I consider running again

I might even sit down

I don't have unlimited kilometres in me

And I've never tested it too far on the treadmill

I know the signs of healthy push and too much push

But WOW

Do I know pretending life is summer

In work

In social life

In house

In travel

In love

Do I ever

Have a transmission

From my glorious little past self
Of burning the candle at both ends
Wondering why I've turned myself into a darned puddle
Cursing myself for cursing myself
But being in too deep
Too many structures already in place
I have to keep going now
And it'll be okay if I just keep going
It's when I stop that the defeat hits
My body screams
Illness takes a front row seat
The rest is forced
And suddenly
It is the middle of summer and my body is protesting the missed winter
*She's in bed*
*She's not getting up*
*The longer she stays in there the worse it gets*
*She's healing*
I can hear the made up judgements of myself
I have been defeated by my own self-enforced perpetual summer
And it's a bit of a shock to the system
To realise the whole world seems structured like this
Perpetual summer
Who cares when the moon is full or dark?
Who is looking at the sunlight, it's time for work?!
Who knows what vegetables naturally grow now, they're just all available?
I've lost the connection

I can't see it
We can't see it
We are in too deep
And the sickness moves us
We tell ourselves
*I will never neglect the appreciation of being able to breathe through my nose*
But I will
Within five minutes
And as soon as I can
I'll be back on the computer,
Back at work,
Minimising the taken sick days,
Regretting using sick days for anything other than holidays,
Ashamed of the clear expression of survival mode,
The cycle starts again
But this is not the natural cycle I was born to
This is not the cycle life begs of me
If I were left alone
This is not how I would live
If I were left alone
I would be a witch
In the forest or by the sea or in the city
I would eat what grew near me
I would appreciate my plate full of food
I would thank the people who loved me by loving them
I would share for I would be plentiful
I would notice the moonlight and want to be in it

I would notice the dark sky and want to be quiet
I would howl at the moon and skinny dip
I would be on my knees for my ancestors
Thanking the witches who were brave enough to share their craft
Willing to stay connected
Courageous enough to tell their stories and even write them down
Thank the witch who told me to soak garlic cloves in honey
And be grateful for the herbs in my garden
That I'd actually know how to use
And if I didn't
It wouldn't matter
Because there would be someone in my village who did
Wait
There is someone in my village who knows
There is someone in your village who knows
There are people in our villages who live this way
And we've judged them
Labeled them as different
Noted it's okay for them but wouldn't be for us because
Excuse
Excuse
Excuse
And we can be that witch
In our way
In our nature
In our summer
And then in our seasons

If only we stop competing with the sun
– Silver is the moon dancing with the sun, not running against it

## SILVER WITCH ROSE

The moon
Is not trying to be the sun
Ruling the day
Lighting up the world
It is the moon
Reflecting light
Sticking to its path
Letting the sun do its thing
– Silver says do *your* thing

Oh dear
Then comes autumn
The one everyone thinks is so pretty
But they are so afraid of it
Why?
It is the season of death
We aren't allowed to talk about death
We fight it
We resist it
We grieve it
We are sheltered from it
We must remember it is not okay to be with it
Only professionals with real training can meet death and be okay
And really honestly they mostly aren't okay
And this is the beginning of our problem with winter,
We cannot rest for we will not die
And we must.
We must let go of who we have been this season
Apply the lessons of this turn of the wheel
Allow what nature has been teaching us to impact us
Allow ourselves to release
Appreciate that a point will come where our elders are no longer with us
We must notice this
For we can't soak in them if we don't appreciate they aren't forever
Even though they are forever
When their bodies are gone we can still speak
It's not the same

It can be very similar

It can even be better

They die and then appear to us healed

Awaken through their transition

It is a great beauty most of us miss

Because we are terrified of autumn

Because we are terrified of silver

We will not let ourselves be as powerful as we are

And we are so surprised when we experience great pain

Death attacks us as if we've never seen it coming

And of course

Shock can be a natural thing

But is it really shocking when health is in such a decline and we can see them slipping away?

It's not always a shock

It's always nature

It's always easier when death is allowed to exist

Literal and emotional

Spiritual and physical

Death is what makes life so precious

So finite and meaningful

So why do we fight it?

If you become okay with death you'll become more invested in life

And that's a vulnerable thing

It is a vulnerable thing to live on the edge of yourself

To change

And grow

And be okay with it

And let go when it's needed
And be with the cycles as they move through you
But give me life with death over life with a blindfold
– Silver knows death is a part of life

We compete

With each other

And ourselves

And our personal expectations

And our image of perfection

And we're doing our best

We don't need to punish ourselves for it

We are human

We are human

Witches are human

– Silver lets us heal as we grow

*'Do your best to connect with where you are right now,'*
*'Do your best to be with nature,'*
*'Do your best to participate in your village,'*
*'Do your best to move towards your vision,'*
*'Know your vision,'*
Silver whispers.
– Silver says steps are better than stagnancy

Summer

Autumn

Winter

Spring

Blooming

Dying

Resting

Reviving

– You are silver

Summer

Autumn

Winter

Spring

Doesn't have to look like

Screaming

Clinging

Surviving

Trying

– You are denying your silver

## SILVER WITCH ROSE

You compete with yourself
When you don't let yourself be
– Let your silver shine

Competition suggests
There is a winner
No witch wins when you suppress her silver
No witch hunter wins either
It's just losers all around
– Loss of silver is a loss of you

## SILVER WITCH ROSE

The thief

Competes with the witch

And it isn't necessary

To steal joy this way

– Silver says ask the village for help, don't fight it

Stop it

– Competing with your silver is over now and if you can just stop pretending that you aren't you, that would be grand

# The defeat of the witch.

The witch didn't realise
She was a witch
For it had been a few generations
And her mother hadn't told her
Her father had kept her a secret
She had no idea
How powerful she was
How connected she was
However, she did know beauty
She looked out the window and longed for it
She could see it in the trees and creatures
Wondered why she could feel so connected to something
She'd been taught wasn't alive
And went about her day
Shrugged it off
Left it at the daydreaming
It was safer that way
– It was safer to hide the silver but it isn't anymore

## SILVER WITCH ROSE

It feels as though

The best thing we can do

When we are scared

Is hide

But actually

It's the hiding

The living in the fear

That puts us in the danger

– Disconnect breeds disconnect, silver breeds love

It was a victory
When the competition was conquered
For a moment
And when it didn't feel so good
No one questioned it
Because what they were meant to do
Was compete and win and celebrate themselves
For dominating another
For coming out on top
But they couldn't shake that feeling
They'd hurt that person
It wasn't a fair game
It wasn't even a joy
Something tickled at their insides
And it didn't make them smile
It made them squirm
They knew, you see
That winning was no triumph
And that they weren't truly free
They were trapped in the same cage
As the loser was perceived
For if they didn't fight that day
They wouldn't be let be
The bullies bully so as to avoid being bullied
The insecure girls scratch to be chosen
The wanting boys force themselves forward
The crops of the neighbour are mysteriously destroyed
It has been happening for centuries

Girls pretending they are women
Boys pretending to be men
Adults; really petty children
This isn't the story's end
There is always a way forward
Perhaps an innocent child who sees
There's more to life, there's magic
There's a way everybody breathes
There's a faltering in the competitors
They don't really want to crush
The villager who lives next to them
To prove they are enough
But they're all scared
They don't know how to leave
This structure that has held them
And taught them how to be
Does anybody know?
Can anybody see?
The competition is over.
There's enough for you and me.
In the background of the fight
A young woman is gazing into the distance
She admires a deer for its beauty
And gasps, when it's gone in an instance
It feels like such a waste,
Such a terror that she's seen
But the hunter wants to share the spoils
With everyone at the scene

And suddenly magic happens
Hearts are opened left and right
And everyone can celebrate
What was an ugly sight
And now the winner and losers
Are all on the same team
They wash in the same river
They drink from the same stream
And soon the village is feasting
Abundance can now be shared
The hunter has begun a remembering
And everybody cared
It took just one to say, *'Let's open,*
*There is another way,'*
And now the floodgates are open
Many offerings are being made
It feels like a new spell
Being woven through the people
They're remembering they're one,
Not millions,
And every one is equal.
The young girl looks to the distance again,
She sees more deer, they are eating,
And she smiles, they're left alone,
The villagers don't need them, they're full
A baby cries, not hungry, just teething
And the hunter comes over
Asks to sit by her side

And she nods, this connection is easy
They fall in love
Generosity in their stride
And become the leaders of these people
– You can't defeat silver

Over and over
And over again
The witches have been squished
Or so you think
Or so it appears
They've never left, though their craft they hid
The witch still knew
Their magic was true
And they knew how to pick their battles
That their time would come
Their blood would live on
And their ancestors would sing with their rattles
– It is no surprise that the women did what they needed to do for the children of their children to know their silver

## SILVER WITCH ROSE

Does it really surprise you
That women are still rising
And witches are still remembering
And you are one of them?
– I am not surprised by your silver

For generations

This has been brewing

You

You have been brewing

A thousand others happened

So you could happen

A thousand betrayals and successes

So you could be here

– You really think all that happened so you could squash your silver?

The village has a pauper
And a wealthy friend
And a big house
And a small farm
And a horse
And a BMW
And a lawyer
And a hippie
And a singer
And a rapper
And an accountant
And a butcher
And a vegan
And a dancer
And a mime
And an actress
And a writer
And a weaver
And I think you get it
– Whoever you are, you are part of the village

When the village separates
And we forget to have each others' back
And we find greed
No longer open to sharing the harvest with our neighbour
Rather watch them struggle from a distance
Than lend a helping hand
Let the elderly man climb on his roof
Pay someone to put the bin out,
Don't ask for gentle help
Suffer
Together
Separately
If we're honest
It won't work
It doesn't work
It doesn't uplift
It doesn't help
It shouldn't surprise us when others want to help
The free women's circle shouldn't be a scam not considered valuable
The price of meat shouldn't stop us cooking dinner
But this reflex has developed
To scan for the disconnect
To assume something is wrong here
Because we can't receive
We've lost the feminine intuition that says
*Receiving is the most important*
*We must receive to know our alignment*
*We must receive before we act*

*We must receive our wisdom*
*We must receive our brothers and sisters*
*We must receive our neighbours*
*We must receive our village*
Because receiving is different to taking
Receiving serves us all
And whilst we live in privilege or not
We must make the best of it all
Someone has to go first
Someone's heart has to open
My neighbour brings us tomatoes
I offer him whisky
They are different things
They mean the same
– The village is easy to receive when we accept our silver

The defeat of the witch
Didn't really happen
– Silver didn't go anywhere

# The discreet witch.

The witch was silenced
Told to stay in her hut
To practice in secret
To share with no one
But she's called to help
She can't help but care
Her hands reach for ointment
Patchouli in her hair
She can't help but offer
Medicine for a child
She can't help but spread her wings
Under the moon she's wild
Slowly but surely
The wild takes hold
Her ability to hide
It's lesser
Slowly but surely
The ways of old
Amaze
Relieve the stressor
Until one day
She says, 'Too much'
And shrinks back to her lonely cauldron
For she is convinced
Enough is enough
She can't be herself any longer
You see the truth is
You're either one with the silver

Or you're doing your best to run from it
Even if you tell yourself you're flying
– If the root says hide the silver eventually you will

It feels so familiar

So safe now

To gather the women in the park

But when I wear my hat

If I pair it with a cloak

*'Halloween is over!'*

He's walking past joking

I'm not laughing inside

But my body laughed

Nervous

Afraid to be seen

Because this is not me for one day a year

This is simply me

This hat tells the village I can heal

This cloak keeps me warm in the elements

I am this witch

This witch is no costume

But he can't see his silver

And people who can't see their silver can be dangerous

It makes me want to run

Take the hat off

Hook the cloak onto a tree and leave it there

Maybe a kid will find a costume

Maybe a witch who can, claim it, will

But just let me be human

Just let me be human

Please let me be human

– Silver *is* human

## SILVER WITCH ROSE

The way you place the candle
The way you flick your hair
The way you lace your dinner with love
The ways you show you care
The ways you raise your mind and heart
The ways you lean in and open
These are the ways of your silver art
A delight, and witch, we are hoping
That you begin to see
The natural way you are
And let yourself express it
That you begin to be
A natural work of art
When silver stops suppression
– You are a witch now

First the silver drips
Breaking the illusion
That it is only for royal spoons
And you realise
Quickly
As you look around the circle
And you peer into the stones
You have done this a thousand times
And you'll do it a thousand more
In the name of remembering
– In circle we remember silver

The circle may be

Humans

Women

Men

Stones

Trees

Lavender bushes

It's less about *what* the circle is

And more that the circle *is*

– Silver dances in the circles we choose

When women gather

Magic happens

We've heard it a million times

When women gather

Bitches rise

You wait, there'll be someone who cries

When women gather

We see the sun

And lift each other up

But if we're broken

Not feeling full

We can leech from each other's cup

As she cries,

Hold her hand not for her,

But for you.

As she screams,

Look around, not to protect her,

But for you.

As she gyrates,

Blush, not for her chastity

But for yours.

As she sings,

Judge, not for her detriment,

But for yours.

*Or...*

Come to the circle

However you are

Open your eyes

If you can't open your heart
Let it be that you are how you feel
Let yourself feel whatever is real
Let yourself cry, feel all your emotions
Let your sisters laugh, let them go through their motions
Let it be chaos,
You aren't all the same
Relate to your sisters,
But live in your own name
Come to the circle
To surrender to the moon
To open to a new best friend
And speak to strangers too
You aren't at the circle
Because you're broken or for a fix
You are here to remember
You are, my dear, a witch
And that means what you make it
Be it brooms and cauldrons and tea
Or simply being one with nature
And singing blessed be
There's no one way to practice your craft
No teacher who can show you the way
But there are plenty of circles filled with love
You'll know, for if you're there you'll want to stay
And not straight away!
Hahaha no
Sometimes you'll arrive

And you'll want to squeal and run all the way home
But eventually
When you break through your crust
When you look into a sister's eyes
Or a candle flame you can trust
Something inside you will open
This magic will peak through the cracks
Suddenly, all the sisters you were hoping
Would appear are here, right on track
Come to the circle
Be a part of the ritual group
And you'll notice that all the woo woo
Is inside your heart too
– A real silver circle feels like home

## SILVER WITCH ROSE

I am the original genius witch
And part of that is a dream
That all around the world there are witches
Hosting silver circles as true queens
And what I really mean by that
Isn't that they're wearing crowns
But that they've put down the need to compete
And they'll see you completely, up and down
For when you can come
To a genius witch circle
You'll remember the magic in your heart
And holding that space
It comes naturally to us
And still, it is a work of art
It's a work of art that I can share
A spell on a page you can keep
And even if you're still a baby witch
And your practice is still quite discreet
I've seen witches hold circle before
With no idea what they're doing
But they come with intention,
With a paper, with a spell
And they're very, very clear in their blessing
They look around the circle
They've invited and others have come
They choose to be of service
And begin to share one by one
And by the time the sharing has come round

The leader knows what to do
It's a dream, to lean in to the sacred intuition,
And if you want it, the dream can come true
If you join The Remembering
And let your heart sing
And build your village
With your sacred offering
It won't take too long
And soon you will find
A coven full of witches
Of every magical kind
They won't all be the same
Won't all tell you the same things
But they'll have the intentions in their hearts
To be natural from summer through spring,
And they'll do their best,
They'll come when they can,
You'll meet new best friends,
You'll come every month,
You'll learn something different
Even if the witches are the same
For every circle changes
To be with the change is the game
It doesn't really matter
How many of you there are
I've sat in the circle alone before
The only witch in the park
Because it takes time

To coax people out
Of their own built illusion
They've forgotten their magic
Prioritised mundane
And may well be drowning in confusion
But give it a chance
Raise your hand, give your heart
You will be amazed to see
The women will come
And if you're a guy, men too
Nature is irresistible you see
There's a reason
The witches content goes so viral
And the average woman has twelve card decks
And the average man can still feel his inner shaman
It's because none of us are average!
We are all filled with magic!
And it's about time we turned up the dial
– Silver is a movement and we must start to build momentum

We must start to build momentum
Even if it's discreet
Even if it's with you and three friends
Otherwise you unconsciously compete
– Gentle silver is better than no silver

A funny thing happens
When you lean into your magic...
... You keep leaning in
– So lean in, silver sage

We
Ignite
The
Circle
Here
– If not you, then who, silver one? (You're lucky if you live in my town)

When I say we ignite the circle
I *really* mean we
Because I will sit in circle a million times by myself
With a crystal and a teddy and a tree
But until you came
It was just a dream
And now we're all in it together
– Silver is for the village

ELLIE ANN DEIGHTON

Silver is for the village
And uplifts the individual
Not, silver is for the individual
With gifts from the village
– Actually it's both

# The teacher witch.

There are the teachers you meet
And there is the teacher you are
And both, if you're lucky,
Will be turned onto the silver
Tapped into magic
Engaged in their nature
Living their true purpose
Sensually alive
Emotionally alchemising
Spiritually attuned
Vocally expressive
Intuitively guided
Soul led
– Luck has nothing to do with it, we choose the silver thread

*'How do you know they're an aligned teacher?'*

They teach you

That means they show you tools

They empower you

They offer you guidance

And even better

They show you the way to your own guidance

You resonate with them

You are challenged to grow by them

They invite you to be self-responsible

They treat you like an adult

They assume you are powerful, not broken and needing fixing

They have kindness in their heart

Not pandering

They are in their own power

Not dictating

They inspire you

And it doesn't have to be exact

They go first in their own way

And encourage you to go first in yours

They let you fly

They hold the space

They have boundaries

They are human and they reveal their flaws

That one's important

They are in the corner of your greatness

And have compassion for your pain

And maybe this isn't a perfect list

But by now you should get the point
– You can feel the silver truth in them

*'How do I know if I'm meant to be a teacher?'*

It will be a calling

You will not shake it

You may hide from it

You may avoid it for a time

But it will come back

Your purpose doesn't dissipate just because you've been distracted

You will come back to the calling

You will hear it again and again

And that is no excuse to wait for later

And not designed to make you feel better for missing it

It simply is.

The calling will come and come.

Your soul will not wait until you are ready.

The day will come when you decide you are ready to not be ready

And then you will teach

And you will improve

And you will learn as you go

And you will be gracious

And you will be impactful

– If teaching is a part of your silver

ELLIE ANN DEIGHTON

You can't get it wrong

Being yourself

And only you can do it

– Your silver cannot be a mistake, cannot be lost, cannot be false

Okay so maybe there is false silver
But is it really false silver
Or is it just false?
– If it ain't nature, it ain't it

In an industry of circles

There is no regulation

And for some this is a problem

But if you think about it

For thousands of years

There have been gatherings

Circles

All-things

Delegations

Festivals

Feasts

Celebrations

Bonfires

Shindigs

Parties

Humans

And they didn't need to be controlled in order to connect

They needed to connect

– Let silver be simple and have a dinner party already

In the village

Everyone is a teacher

Everyone is in their special gifts

Everyone does not have to learn everything

You can be in your lane

You can share your magic

You can witness others in their lane

You can be in their magic

In the village

Silver is moving through us all

The moon wakes us all up when it's brightest and highest

The sun reminds us all that we are alive

The stars inspire us all

The fire warms us all

The breeze cools us all

The flowers heal us all

The Earth sings to us all

We all become bones

– Getting silver yet?

It doesn't matter what you believe

It matters how you live

– Silver shines in all seasons

Silver is

The ultimate all-season spire

Permission to be yourself

A relief to not have to know

A beast when you need it

Why you are so big

And so small

And so important

And so meaningless

Silver is

Your freedom

And your own prison if you won't learn it

– Learn your silver with your people

Your people

Are your village

Your teachers

Your friends

Your confidants

The women and men in your circle

The queers in your circle

The animals in your circle

The plants in your circle

The allies in your circle

The lovers in your circle

The mountains in your circle

It's all your village

– Give silver to the village and the village will give silver back

## SILVER WITCH ROSE

Silver is abundant

So you can teach it

And give it away

And express it

And charge for it

And whatever

And there will always be more

And you will always be you

And no one will ever be able to replicate it

For no one else will ever have your silver

No one else will ever hold the circle like you do

And everyone can

– No silver is equal and all silver is equal

ELLIE ANN DEIGHTON

Silver is not about equality
It is about harmony
It isn't about balance
It is about alignment
– We want silver to flow, not barter

You don't need to force
Your silver to come out
If you pause
Breathe
Regulate that beautiful nervous system of yours
Let yourself have
Summer, autumn, winter, spring
You will become the expression of your silver
You will have to show up
But you won't have to try
I ask my silver about my health
And my heart simply whispers, *'Move'*
And I do have to show up and move
But I don't have to try to be anything other than me
I simply move the body I am living in
And more and more of my silver reveals itself
And that is one example
Out of a thousand million trillion
But you get it, right?
You show up for yourself
And your silver will teach you
Remind you
You will remember
*This* is how you love
*This* is how you love to move
*This* is how you spellcast
*This*
*This*

*This*

Is a silver teaching witch

She is learning as she moves

He is guided by his heart

They are one with their unique processes

Choosing to be themselves

That's the point, witch

– The true teacher witch is simply being their silver self

Witch

Has been a word of heavy definition

For a long time

When I say, 'Witch'

You think what?

When I say, 'Witch'

You feel what?

When I call you, 'Witch'

You respond how?

When I call myself a witch

You judge how?

Actually answer the questions.

Yes, for real.

Okay now...

These are your definitions

This is your opportunity

Keep them or change them?

– You can be a teacher witch right now

The witch
Who burned in the village
For placing her fingers in the soil
And sighing
Singing
To bountiful crops
That she would have shared
Were she not burned...
She can be a teacher witch for you if you let her.
The wife who lived next door to her
Who let her burn
Who seethed with jealousy
Who knew in her heart there was no evil there
Can be a teacher witch for you.
The man who strung her up
Who cheered as she was tortured in her cage
Who lit the fire with his instruction
Who held no grace and felt only the joy of defeating her threat to his monopoly
He can be a teacher witch for you.
– Just because they have silver, doesn't mean they are living it, doesn't mean you can't learn from them, doesn't mean you can't live yours, doesn't mean they were a 'good' witch

## SILVER WITCH ROSE

I don't know if I believe in good witches
But I believe in hearty witches
And you can tell the difference
Between a witch being filled from their heart
And a witch hunting for their heart as if it's outside of them
– I know which witch I wanna be

# The evil witch.

Bet

I

Taste like

Charcoal to

Her

– Just because my silver love burns her tongue it doesn't mean she isn't worth loving

She hates me

Or so I think

But she could love me

For all I know

I just can't see past the stink

Of the sister wound

The witch wound

The pain I'm meant to be living in

Can you?

– As soon as I intend to see past it, I can because the silver shines

It's not just she

Who has twisted magic

It's him too

Them

Everyone

We all twist it

We all corrupt it

We all forget about it

We all disrupt it

We all build amazing momentum and then pull the plug

We all try 'our best' and fail, knowing we could have been more invested

We all fuck up sometimes

And the wheel turns

– The silver doesn't disappear

Evil is a concept

A belief

A definition

To experience

If you choose

Or you can use silver to your advantage

And live a life aligned with nature

And give zero fucks about what anyone calls it

Because it's not good or bad

Or right or wrong,

It's just you being yourself

– Stop being so mean to yourself and each other, silver one

Evil witches

Haunt dreams

Ruin Halloween

Suck reverence

– And you don't have to buy into it if you buy into your own silver

## SILVER WITCH ROSE

You are your best investment
Everyone says it
Are you listening yet?
– What are you doing about your silver?

The evil isn't external
It isn't someone else coming to get you
You don't need to run from it
You need to shine
Be so damn magnetic in your magic that evil bows down and says,
'*Okay, teach me how to love*'
– There's love and silver and then there's everything else, call it what you want

# The wise witch.

We all have wisdom
Every single one
And sometimes we know it
But sometimes we play dumb
Sometimes we don't want to ask for help
It's the silliest thing we can do
Because then we strive to do it all ourselves
And sure enough, tiredness breaks through
It's an arrogant thing
Half-wise at best
To believe we know it all
To be afraid of saying
For we might fail a test!
We've no idea at all
– Silver isn't for it's own expense, it's for the truth

When you come to the circle
You'll meet a high priestess
And as if by chance, you'll look in her eyes
But it's not by chance
It's on purpose
She's looking and when she sees you, you're surprised
Because she doesn't simply see you
She sees through
The masks you've been wearing to hide
And the pain
And the facade
And the fake
And the know it all
And the not knowing what to do
And the fight of giving up, going alone
And the wisdom that you've come here to wash in
And the heart that called you here
And the love you have to share
And the magic in your heart
And the season that you're in
And the season that's your best essence
She sees through
Anything you think you want her to see
And all she sees
Is who you are beneath
– Silver in one sees silver in all

It is difficult to describe
The sense of magic
One feels
All feel
In the circle
So I want you to imagine
Really try
Imagine I can articulate it!
Imagine you walk into a candlelit room
And there are twelve other people there
All strangers
All connected
And you feel nervous
Maybe a little socially anxious
Maybe a little excited
Maybe you're berating yourself for thinking coming here was a good idea
Maybe you're wondering if anyone will notice if you leave
(They will)
Maybe you are loving it and terrified at the same time
How would you feel?
Walking into that room?
There's a circle of cushions, one for each bum
Chairs on the edges of the room for anyone who needs them
Candles on every available surface
It's warm, a good level of warm
It smells fantastic
Aromatherapy to relax (lavender) and connect you to your heart (rose)

In the middle of the circle there's an altar

It may not mean much to you yet

But there is magic in there

You can feel it

You brought something with you to place in the middle

*'Charge up your special item in our group centre'*

The invitation said

So you brought the first thing that jumped into your mind

(What did you bring?!)

The leader steps into the centre and places an item down,

A photo

And you take that as an invitation

So does everybody else

To place your item in

You witness

A watch

A crystal

A book

A bracelet

A ring

Another photo

A kid's toy

A bunch of seemingly random items being placed in a now slightly messy altar

But it's good mess

It feels perfectly imperfect

You notice your shoulders relax

Not that you noticed yourself tensing them

And the leader sits down
So you sit next
And everyone takes their place
And there is silence
Everyone taking a breath
The leader takes a really deep breath and looks around
When she looks into your eyes...
You've never felt so welcome
In an instant she has said,
*'Hello!*
*Welcome!*
*I am so glad you are here'*
And hugged you in her warm embrace
*'Well done'*
And congratulated you for overcoming your resistance
For following the call of your heart and arriving
And you know you're where you're meant to be
And she starts speaking
And you are listening
And the more she speaks, the more you know
*This is the right space for me*
The more she shares, the more you know
*She is my type of people*
The more she breathes, the more your body relaxes
– And so you receive a silver welcome

## SILVER WITCH ROSE

Now the circle opens
You take a deep breath
You are sat across from the head witch
So there's space before it's your turn
Everyone is sharing
Everyone is sharing their name, how they're feeling
And the intention in their heart,
*I don't know what to say!*
You may be thinking to yourself,
But you don't have to know what to say,
Right now it's your role to listen,
Soak up the other women
As they share,
Lean into receiving them,
In their hearts
*'I want to make new friends'*
*'I love it every time I come'*
*'I really just needed some time with other adults'*
*'I really needed time to myself'*
*'I love to be around people who help me expand and you are that'*
*'I want to reconnect with the wild woman in me'*
*'I have seen my husband love men's work and I wanted the women'*
Or maybe for the men in the back
*'I have seen my wife love women's circles and I wanted to suss out the men'*
*'I'm feeling so good and inspired!'*
*'I'm so nervous and hearing you all share makes me feel so much better'*
*'I don't know why I'm here, I just knew I had to be'*

And when your turn comes you know exactly what to say
*'Hi, my name is...'*
*'My heart is feeling...'*
And you'll pause for a moment to really feel and share
*'My intention for this evening is...'*
And the perfect answer will come
And this is how we call forth our wisdom
We begin
We start the sentence
We accept the invitation
We arrive
We show up
We listen
We take our turn
We have a go
We express ourselves
We share our truth
We do our best
We learn when it doesn't go how we wanted
We learn when it goes better than expected
And then we repeat
– Silver is a cycle, not a one stop shop

# The silver witch rose.

You've been coming for a while now
Attending the circles
Answering the call
Lighting the candles
Pulling the cards
Setting the boundaries
Making the love
Having the orgasms
Riding the waves
Sharing your vulnerability
Writing in your journal
Offering your reflections
Realising you have wisdom
Making new connections
Redefining old relationships
Sitting in the circle
Bringing the circle home with you
Letting the intentions light you up
Being guided by nature
Noticing the moon
Receiving the gifts of the cycles
Reverently bleeding
And all of a sudden
One day
It just happens:
You bloom.
– The silver witch in you has been there all along

ELLIE ANN DEIGHTON

# Queen Of The Stones
## The Epilogue

*Many, many thousands of years ago...*

They walked softly over the long winter grass
The rain had warmed the earth
They were not afraid of the elements and although their feet would eventually freeze
They knew they would soon be dancing in the ritual
And soon
They would not care nor feel any pain
They were dressed in robes
Decorated with ropes and furs
All made by hand
All produced by the village
Some supported by staffs
Most simply allowing themselves to move at their own gentle pace
There's no hurry
This is a walk of great reverence
It is a visit to the stones
They can see them in the distance
They have travelled far to see them
To be here
Secret rites of passage are about to unfold
No one knows who the centre of the ritual will be
They don't need to know
They know they will arrive and the land will speak to them
They will be moved
There will be a ritual

A dance
A spirit will move through their very bodies
And they will let it
They will be sparked with visions and songs
And they will let them move them
They will witness themselves as the vessel
They will witness each other
They understand it's all a reflection
A message for all of them
A foretelling of the path before them if they do not change
A fortune from the stars
Whispers from the moon
They aren't sure
Though they are sure they will know when it comes
The humming begins
The song starts
It ripples through gently
There's no need for heavy catharsis
It is not dramatic
It is an opening
The body shakes and moves
Then there is a graceful dance
A man who needs his staff to walk, drops it and rolls
Then stands effortlessly as the spirit connects him
A woman who is about to give birth moves more gracefully than the sea
The youngest laughs
A spirit of joy moving through the field

They are all youth
They are all elders
They are all everything
They are all nothing
They are here for the stones
But really they are here for each other
For themselves
For the remembering that comes
When we gather in reverence
And we let nature move us
Showing us that we were all one all along
And that even though our dances are unique
Individual and separate
We are all a part of the same village
And we are all across all of space and time
The remembering is fleeting
And the remembering is forevermore
– Silver is timeless

# salt sugar spirit
## out september 2025

### A pinch of SALT

Deep in the cauldron of your body
There is an essence
That cannot be hidden from
Nor removed
It cannot be changed
Nor corrupted
It cannot be tainted
Nor broken
Through all of life's transformation
And every metamorphosis
This essence is with you
This essence will never let you down
Even if you ignore it
This essence will call to you
Even if you defy it
This essence will lovingly guide you
Even if you deny it
This essence will wait

Even if you defile it
This essence will be complete and okay
Even if you wish you never had it
This essence will never cease to love you on your path
Even if you are consumed by dogma
Even if you are afraid of it
Even if you are told it is wrong
Even if you are conditioned away from it
Even if you forget
You can burn
You can burn
You can burn
And the spirit is right there
– The salt of your soul isn't going anywhere

Your salt is calling you. Will you listen?
Read ***Salt Sugar Spirit*** from September 2025

# About the author

She teaches humans how to live in the light of their true selves and she goes first.
Like an integrity radar
Through life
Hers and yours
She will find the cracks
And spit them out
Until your world tastes like honey together
For she is not here to walk alone
And neither are you.
It is no mistake that you are here reading this.
Is it stories in her books calling you in for a journey?
Is her music singing you home to the temple of you?
Is her curriculum asking you to become more of yourself?
Is now the time?
I believe so.
The scientist in her has a hypothesis,
That you are magic,
The facilitator in her
Can prove it,

The witch in her

Can give you the tools to cast it,

The woman in her

Can celebrate you as you shine,

The artist in her

Is on stage creating beside you.

You are magic,

And here,

You will find that you are home.

– about Ellie, author of ***Silver Witch Rose***

# Author's note

You are never alone
Because you will always have your silver
And silver will always be inside you
And you can close your eyes and see the silver
And you can open your eyes and look for the silver
And you can place your hands on your body and feel the silver
And you can sing a song and hear the silver whisper
And even on the darkest days
There can be a light
Because of the silver
And the greatest gift you could ever give yourself
Is to learn to

See

Listen

Feel

Receive

Remember

Play

Speak

Be

Silver
– Silver is what I teach


And I can teach you to remember your silver too
Or you can receive little silver drops to your inbox

Subscribe to 'Silver' at [elliedeighton.com/silver](elliedeighton.com/silver)

# The Remembering
## The Silver Circle Personal Invitation

In the forest,
There is a whisper
And you can hear it
If you listen
It's like a drum beat
It's calling you
To move your feet
It's calling you
To bring you home
It's calling you
To the ways of old
It's calling you
And if you are willing
You can join us
Every month
Every moon
Every seasonal shift
Everywhere on the planet
To walk home to your calling

To make space for your remembering
For when you make the space to listen
When you make the space to receive
When you self care in the new moon
Self create with the seasons
And self release with the full moon
You will remember the magic in your heart
And when you have that remembering
You will be called forth to share yourself
Your truest self
And you will be yourself
And really
That is the real mission of this life.

Join Ellie for live and pre-recorded rituals, meditations and sound journeys and find your magic in your heart.
elliedeighton.com/thesilverremembering

# Acknowledgements

Clare
Mem
William
BeAta
Merrian
Nicholas
John
Lydia
Elissa
Layard
Geoff
Craig
Kirsty
Jane
Nan
Zaylee
Faith
Devin
Paige
CJ

Lenian

Urs

Tom

Timothy

– Thank you for your magic, ***Silver Witch Rose*** wouldn't exist without you

www.ingramcontent.com/pod-product-compliance
Lightning Source LLC
Chambersburg PA
CBHW071243070526
44583CB00017B/2308